LANDSCAPE IN TEXTILES

Hand-dyed fabric collages of landscapes in the south of England

Kate Findlay

©2020

Introduction

This book is a collection of some of the landscapes I have made in fabric. I started making these pictures about five years ago. It grew out of the journal quilts I made on a bird theme, which in turn had started as a means of expressing myself in a very different way having spent nearly five years working on my large Hadron Collider series!
I enjoyed the freedon of raw edge applique, just collaging fabrics to make compositions. When I look back on earlier pictures I see how little stitching I added, letting the colours and shapes speak for themselves. Now I find I work into the picture a lot more, perhaps because my confidence has grown with the free motion embroidery.

I work from my studio, which has a long workbench set to my height. Above it there is a pinboard for pinning up work - and also for taking photos of them when they are finished. I have my Juki machine set up permanently on another table, and there is storage underneath for boxes of fabric and all the usual clutter!

Fabric techniques

Much of my fabric is hand-dyed. Above is a photograph of some gradation dyeing, where I start with two different dye colours (one at each end) and dilute them as I work across the six tubs. This gives me sets of fabrics which work well together but are all a bit different.

I have been adding other techniques to the repertoire too, and you will see examples where I have used thickened procion dyes painted onto white cotton as a background. I sometimes print and stamp added textures into the backgrounds to create more complexity and depth.

When I collage the fabric I always prepare it first with a fusible - Bondaweb is my preferred choice. I take off the backing paper and then cut shapes and iron them. I always machine stitch on top, and finally stretch the work over a board and lace the back, before sending to my framer. I also use UV glass as it protects the fabric further.

Stormy Skies

These two pieces were driven by the hand-dyed fabric used in the sky. It cried out to be used as a dramatic sky, and then it seemed a logical follow on to use bright yellows, indicating fields of rape, which are common around Oxfordshire. I have always loved that amazing but fleeting impression you get after a storm of brilliant sunlight against a menacing sky.

Storm over Streatley shows a road which runs from Blewbury to Streatley in Oxfordshire which twists and turns through beautiful countryside. Roads are not particularly pretty, but it was such an important part of the composition it had to be included, and of course Hockney has used roads in a number of his large paintings, so this is my homage to his style of work!

Storm over Streatley
50cm x 50cm

Storm Clearing

Bluebell woods

I adore bluebell woods and always try and get out to see some each year. We are fortunate around Berkshire and Oxfordshire as there are some really good ones.

It is a subject that I have re-visited a few times as it is always so beautiful. The blue of bluebells is the prettiest colour on earth!

Hand-dyeing is a great way to get the subtlety of the colours and the changes from light to dark which occur with dappled sunlight. In these two pieces I have tried to simplify the shapes to allow the colours to dominate. Once I have the basic structure of the piece I do a lot of free cutting of leaf shapes, tucking some under the tree trunks to create more depth. The free-motion stitching afterwards pulls it all together, and is particularly useful for creating the smaller twigs and background trees.

Harpsden Wood

Afternoon Light

This scene was inspired by a lovely visit to the Vyne - a National Trust property near Basingstoke. I was really struck by the quality of light streaming through the horse chestnut trees, with the darker shadows in the foreground.

Painting the background

"Afternoon Light" is a combination of techniques. The background started as plain white soda soaked delphina cotton, pinned out flat. In the photo above you can see the trays of procion dye, thickened with manutex paste. This is painted, sponged and scraped on and then left to cure before being washed out.

The photo to the left shows the same piece, noticeably lighter having been washed and dried. All the foreground is collaged on top. The leaves and grass texture are created with small pieces cut up and sprinkled over a very lightweight fusible web, then ironed and stitched.

Afternoon Light

By the River

The tranquil Loddon is a tributary of the Thames and holds a special place in my heart. I have walked beside it and canoed down it many times and never tire of the miniature vistas round every bend in the river filled with interesting plants and shy wildlife.

This piece is quite sizeable at nearly 80cm across, and was challenging as a study in greens. it certainly makes you look at nature more closely when you are trying to work out how to make the reflections look convincing! Still water in sunshine often has that slightly milky quality which means the reflections are slightly lighter than the trees above.

Walking the Loddon

Reflections I

This pair of pieces was made soon after "Walking the Loddon". I really wanted to explore the whole reflection theme further. It pushed me to think carefully about the textures I was creating as well as the many shades of green needed to create the work. It is very satisfying when you find a piece of fabric that works perfectly, and that happened with the fabric which forms most of the water in the right side of the picture. (left)

The swatches above are taken from some of the gradation dyeing I did to create a palette of related colours for this project.

Reflections II

The reflections were again, challenging, as sometimes the water is opaque, but at other times it is clear, creating further colours in the depths.
The piece above is a small study on the river margin - I enjoy creating the layers of reflections overlaid with the lilypads.

Hidden Pool

The shape of the trees across the bright pool attracted me to make this piece. I love collage, but it has its limitations, and I was looking to achieve a more painterly feel in the picture.

With the help of InStitches studio (based near Wokingham), I learnt how to mix and apply a thickened procion dye in a manutex carrier. You can see trays of this in the earlier work Afternoon Light.

It is a slightly awkward method of working, as you need to apply the colour darker than you want it to be, and also need to leave the fabric rolled in plastic overnight to cure, before washing out all the manutex paste thoroughly, and drying the fabric. I don't always get it right and have needed several overdyeing sessions to get the effect I require.

Work in Progress

The photo above shows the background painted with dye on stretched delphina cotton. I worked from a sketch but ignored all my foreground detail.

The picture bottom left shows how I have overlaid tracing paper onto my now dry background, so I can draw in the tree shapes using charcoal. I used this to form templates for my tree trunks, cut out of pre-bonded fabric. Smaller details could then be added with free cutting and stitching.

Sometimes I still don't get the colour balance right, and have to collage more dyed fabric in certain parts of the picture to make it work how I want, but I do try not to overwork it.

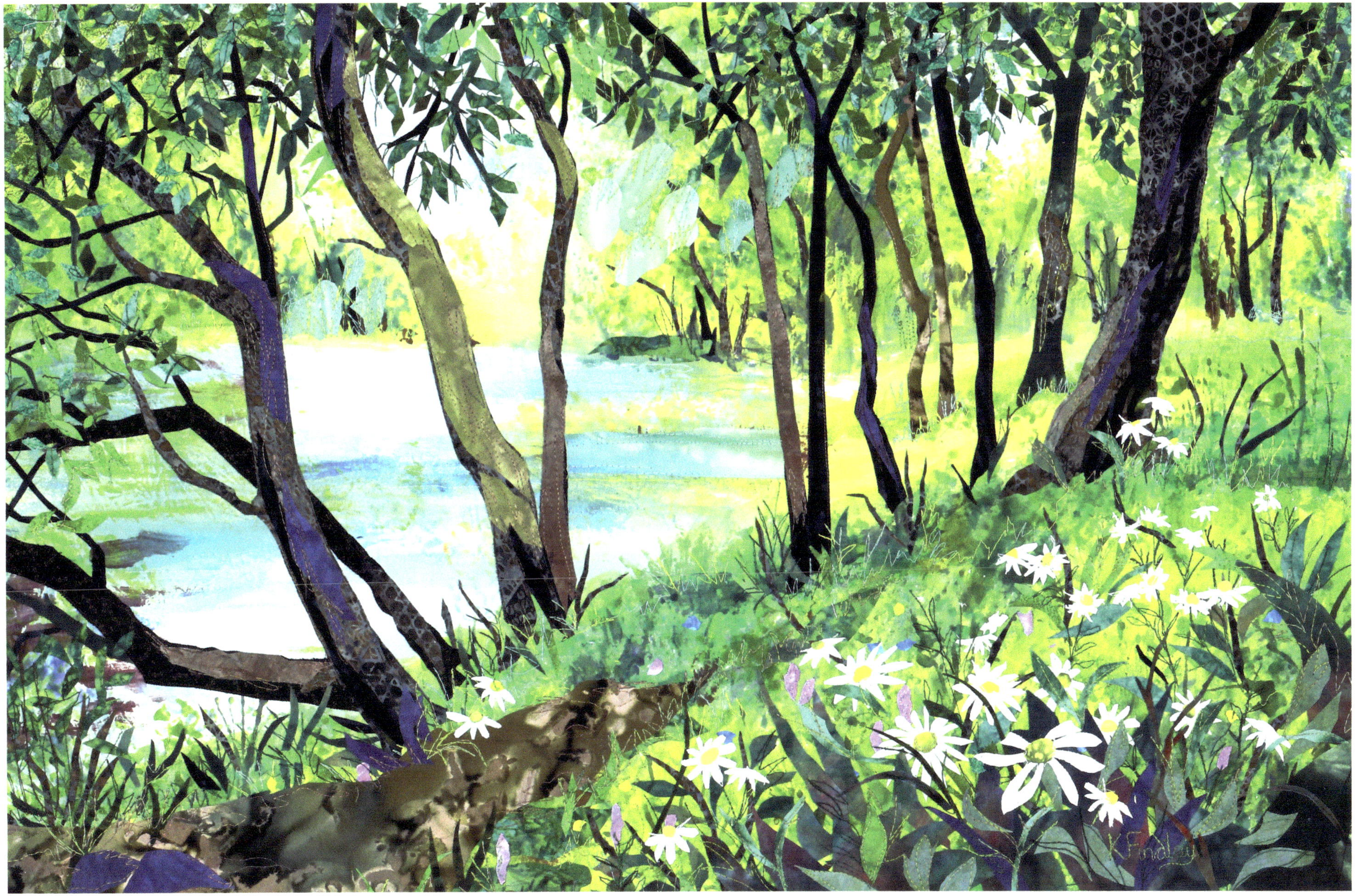

The Ridgeway

I have done a number of pieces inspired by the Ridgeway which is about an hour's drive from where we live. It transports you back in time when walking this ancient track with few cars or houses to be seen. In late summer it is characterised by huge rolling fields of buttery yellow corn, big skies and the white chalk of the path underfoot. I love this empty brightness and sound of birdsong on the wind.

Ridgeway Rambling
This piece is about 50cm square and is purely collaged from pre-bonded fabrics.

The White Horse

I go looking for inspiration in a large radius around Reading. The White Horse of Uffington is an iconic landmark in the South of England, and one that I was keen to attempt in fabric. The tricky problem however is that from the ground it is impossible to see the entire horse in any useable form, so a degree of artistic licence is required.

The other major factor for me is the scale of the landscape and trying to get across the airy space and interesting folds in the hills. I have used machine stitching to help to define the contours of the land. The foreground has some fabric paint added to recreate the pale grasses on the downs and also to emphasise the chalkiness of this landscape.

The White Horse

Avebury Standing Stones

The mystery of these ancient stones needed a rather unual approcah to colour. The fabric is all hand-dyed, and I was keen to try something different in the sky, settling on this pink fabric. Sometimes it is different lighting conditions or certain times of day - early morning, late evening, or perhaps a storm which brings a landscape alive. I like to sketch out compositional ideas to clarify the proportions of a piece before starting. I used this long rectangular format for a number of the pieces in this book. This work is about 80cm wide.

Avebury Standing Stones

Wittenham Clumps

This popular beauty spot in Oxfordshire is a very attractive place with wonderful views across the countryside. I wanted to really capture the bones of the place - the underlying structure that makes the hills so interesting. We went there on a blowy day in late Autumn and the trees were bare, but I still love the shapes they create. I am inspired by the work of John Nash, and you might recognise echoes of his tree shapes in the way I have treated my trees.

Thumbnail sketches and photographs are used to help work out composition. People create interest but need to be quite distant.

Wittenham Clumps

Out Sketching

Hambledon Mill is on the Thames a couple of miles downriver from Henley-on-Thames. I went out on a lovely crisp frosty day to gather inspiration for some new work. Sunny days are so much better for taking photos as the colours are brighter, and shadows can be used to advantage in creating more interesting compositions.

Hambledon Mill

The mill is set on the north bank of the Thames, but I approached it from the southern side, parking at Remenham. It is a dramatic place, with a considerable length of weirs and walkways over the water. It is also spread out over quite a distance which makes composition tricky. I wanted to try and condense the action into a square format, so I had to be creative with some of the angles and perspectives.

When I was taking the photos, the sun was quite low and inevitably, some of the more interesting shots ended up being into the sun. When I looked at these however, I was really struck by the distinct colour palette of blacks, a range of blues and white, and wanted this to feature in the finished work.

As I had already been creative with the actual composition, I went a step further and created stylised swirls where the water was roaring out of the weir gates.

The City Watcher

I made this piece for a competition run by the RSPB. It was about raising awareness of attracting swifts back into the centre of Oxford, and immediately touched a chord with me. I really like our bird life and am concerned about the way a lot of common birds are just disappearing, but also I really fancied attempting an urban landscape.

I played around with a number of ideas for the composition - square and long formats, but also with the viewpoint too. It seemed appropriate to be looking down on the city as this was about birds, but I have also had a long standing love of gargoyles, which led to a rather worried looking gargolye becoming the focus of this picture.

The colour palette was also a concious decision as I wanted to get that rather misty effect of early mornings, but bringing in the wonderful sandy colours of the Oxford stone too.

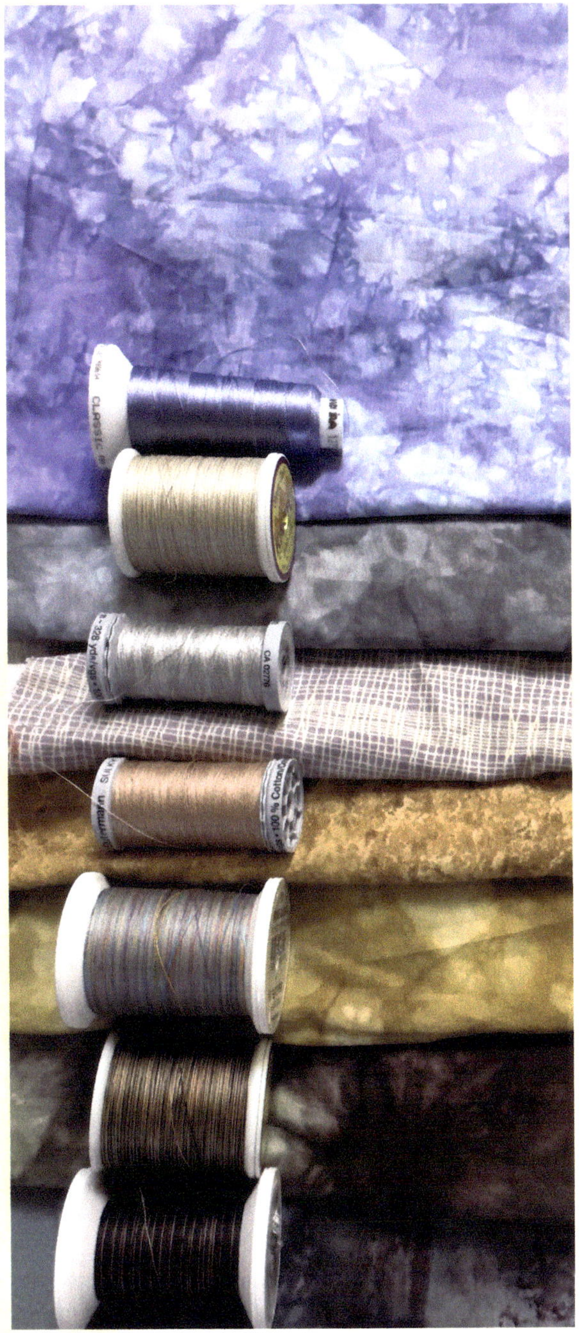

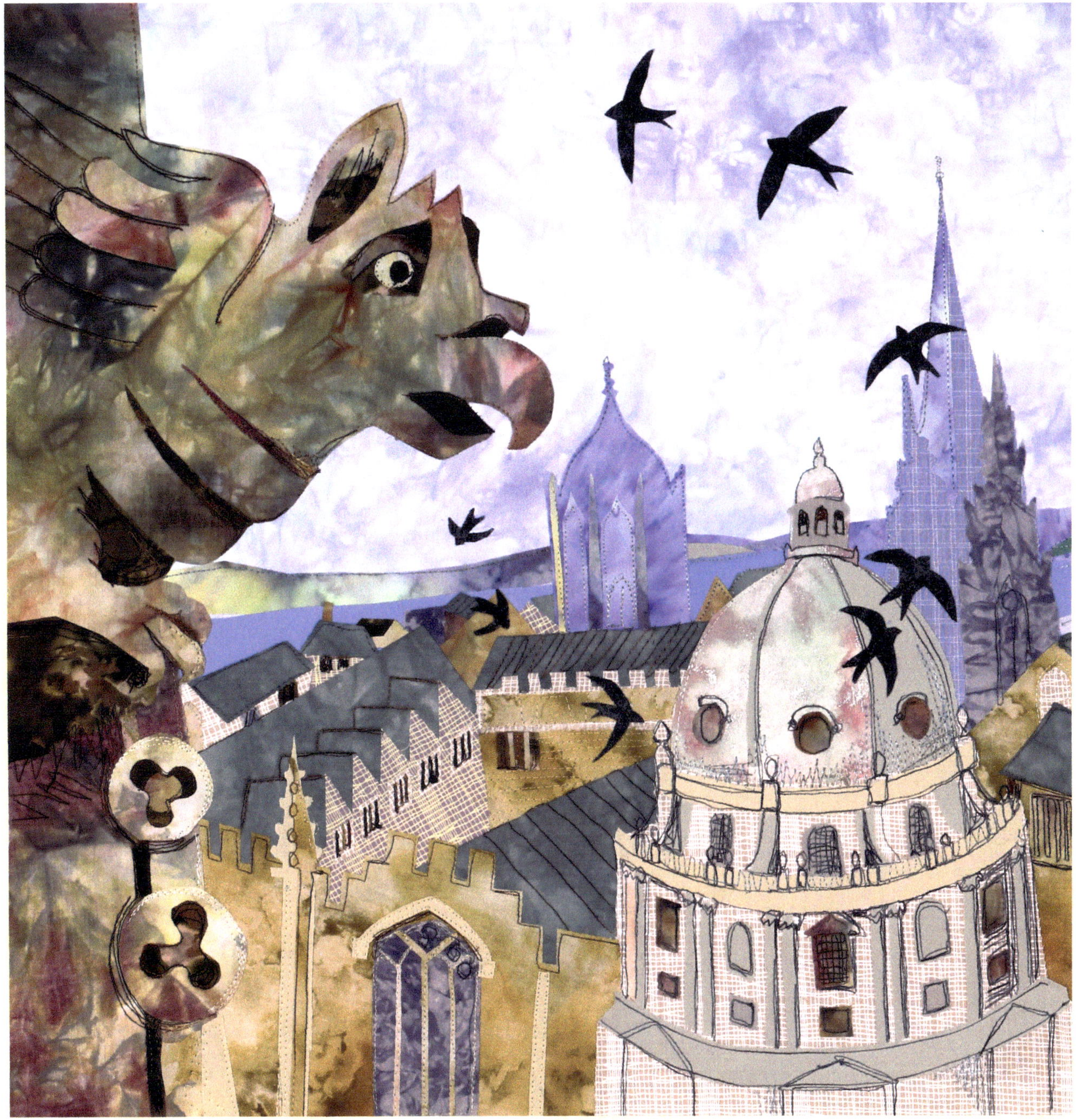

Temple Island

Temple Island is downriver from Henley-on-Thames, and is known as the starting point for many of the Henley Regatta races. It is very picturesque, and makes for a very pleasant walk along the Thames. I have visited it many times over the years and have two versions in fabric here. The one bottom right was inspired by a fabulous frosty morning walk before I was due to teach a workshop in the nearby Remenham village hall. I was very struck by the subtle colour palette of pale blues and greys.

Serene temple Island (right)
is more autumnal, but both had the huge challenge of creating the effect of the mist across the water. I achieved this with layers of sheer fabrics held down with some tiny handstitching. Having a good variety of fabric in light shades also helped with the transition across the water.

Serene Temple Island

Autumn Landscapes

My favourite time of year - as long as there are more crisp sunny days than windy wet ones! I can think of nothing better than a long woodland ramble swishing through crunchy fallen leaves. The small piece on the left was exploring the shape of the shadows on the field and also using perspective to help create a sense of space and distance in the picture.
Autumn Splendour also uses the shadows as an important part of the composition creating horizontal stripes which contrast with the verticals of the trees.

Commercial batik fabrics can be useful, and the piece on the left has some of these in it. However, the joy of using hand-dyed fabrics is the wonderful textures and accidental marks you get with tray dyeing, where the whole point is *not* to end up with flat colours. I have a plentiful stash, but what I find interesting is that nothing goes to waste. I might reject a piece of fabric for one picture - maybe it was too orange, too bright? - only to find it is just perfect for another project. Very satisfying!

Autumn Splendour

Winter river

A bright day in January gave me the opportunity to take some photos of this local river, and I was immediately inspired to make these two pieces. I had been playing with a new app on my ipad called Imaengine, which transforms photos in interesting ways. I found it helped to simplify the shapes and colours and I wanted to keep the rather graphic and slightly abstract style in the work.

Blackwater 1
I particularly wanted to make marks with the fabric which were reminiscent of lino cutting. This was inspired by the simplified version of this photo which I had played around with in Imaengine. The machine stitching on top was quite free and scribbly.

Blackwater 2
Above is the altered photo run through Imaengine which helped me to make this piece. I drew out the design actual size but did quite a lot of improvised cutting of pre-bonded fabrics.

Wren and Rosehips

These two pieces are approximately 35cm square. I made them specifically as greeting card designs as I licence work to various companies. Having done a number of bird and animal pictures I noticed that popular designs had a landscape behind the bird.

I make templates for specific shapes such as the house, bird and branches, and pin these to my chosen fabrics. I assemble the collage and iron everything down before finishing it with free motion machine stitching to complete the details of trees, twigs and the berry ends.

Blackbird and Crabapples

I watch a blackbird in my garden eating the crabapples, which gradually gets harder to do as he pecks off all the accessible ones first. The threatening sky makes a lovely contrast with the snow, and the bare branches make attractive shapes, framing the imaginary cottage.

I make a number of preliminary sketches - some very rough thumbnails - and draw a number of birds before firming up the design. This one originally had a thatched cottage but it felt too fussy.

I really enjoyed designing these pieces with a limited colour palette and thinking how to introduce that necessary flash of seasonal colour!

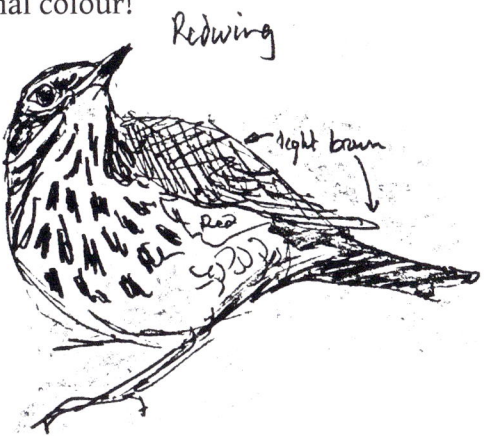

Arts FINDLAY
textiles

Kate is a textile artist and teacher. She taught art in primary and secondary schools for many years before going self employed in July 2018. She now spends her time making and exhibiting textile pieces such as the ones in this book, as well as travelling the country giving talks and workshops to wonderful groups of people who have an interest in textiles. You can find more of her work on her website, and she also has videos on YouTube showing the construction of some of her work. Find her on Facebook and Instagram too where she posts regular updates about her work and shows.

Facebook/Instagram : @artsfindlay

Website: www.artsfindlay.co.uk